MW01253234

Satsang Poetry

No part of this book may be used or reproduced in any manner without permission of the author.

Published in the U.S.A.

ISBN 13
978-1470174224

ISBN-10
1470174227

Table of Contents

Table of Contents

Table of Contents

Table of Contents

A Rage of Angels

Wings, wet with tears
Made rigid with anger
Tattered and torn from battle
Are not flight worthy

Dashed against the rocks
Thrown helplessly to the ground
When such an angel
Looks up and sees another
Soaring with grace
Held by the wind
Trusting the air itself
Seeking the warmth of the sun
Joyous and free
Bound to the Earth no more
This is when she dries her tears
Climbs the mountain once more
And stands on the ledge

But this time
Instead of pushing the wind
Demanding her right to fly
She simply asks
That it carry her home
And let her sleep among the clouds.

All that you need do
Is let her see you soar
That will be enough
Let her see you soar

Butterfly Effect

The butterfly flaps its wings
Because it is its nature
And what is its nature
But its essence
From which it cannot hide

Must it ground itself
In fear and shame
And shed a tiny tear
In seeing what has become
Of it's own expression?

The breeze turns
Ever so slightly downward
And gently kisses the Earth
In a way that would not have been
And joins more of it's kind
Racing skyward in wanton lust
To feel itself
Against the rustling leaves

And does it gasp in horror
In idle witness to what follows
Or is it just a playful breeze
Seeking the wonder
Of becoming a storm?

As gales rage and swirl
And trees are toppled
and heaven darkens with fury
Is there one apart
Who can raise a hand
And declare in anger
Or noble indignation
'Cease! What is, must not be!'

There is no such a one
Amidst the swirling orgasm
Of creation and destruction
And it doesn't matter

Is the clap of thunder
That shakes the bed
And awakens the sleeper
......A mistake
No, rather it is an awakening
That softens the arrogance
Of the hapless sleeper
Who in his slumber
Would stand apart from the
Storm
And silence its nature
As though he had one
Of his very own

Let it be what it is
For we know how to awaken
From our own nightmares

Now I Know

It humbles me beyond humility
To the greatness that I Am

It breaks my heart
And cracks it open
So that it can hold infinity

It's trying to kill me
That I may be born
It's ripping me apart
that I may be whole

I know this longing
As I know myself
Which is to say
I know nothing

Love destroys before it gives life
My God! I didn't know that

Harmony

I've walked the rain kissed earth
And breathed deeply the bitterness of winter's slumber
I've dodged the angry pelting hurls of heaven
That moisten my face to reflect the treachery beneath my feet
That seeks to bring me to my knees in humble resignation

I've braced the bitter winds that seek out my vulnerable places
To extinguish the light that burns within

I paused to turn my back to the fury
As I contemplated a single bird in no such struggle
Hovering effortlessly and motionless in the stiff, cold breeze
Without reason seeking only the glory of it's own power of flight
In perfect joy and harmony
Oblivious to the tortures of nature that were mine alone

And so it is that as I struggle
Against a nature that is my own beauty and wonder
I once again reach out to touch the face of God

Small Wonder

I see the anger in their hearts
The pain in their faces
The hate in their voices
I see angels crawling
Warriors cowering
Gods begging on the streets

I see children dying
And futures fading to black
I see the wisdom of age
Alone and forgotten
Unheard, lost forever

I see nature endlessly giving
Bending to the weight
Of our greed and arrogance

Small wonder I'm filled with sadness
What sorcery is this
That clips the wings of angels
And makes fools of Gods?

How is it that all roads lead to heaven
And we are so very lost?

Listen to Me

You don't understand me
I no longer want what you have to give
Can you make me safe enough
That I will at last be free?
Can you teach me enough
That I will know what you do not?
If I let you fill my life with things
Will you also fill my heart with joy?
Can you fly me fast enough
To escape the baggage I carry with me?
Can you fly me high enough
To touch the face of God?

Then I have no use for you
For something calls me
From beyond the borders
Of your well built walls
Your placid smiles
Your rules and rites of passage
Your insincerity and your apathy

There is a peace so absurd
That you won't hear of it
There is wonder and beauty so awesome
That you cannot own it
And so you do not see it
There is love so deep
That it would bring you to your knees
And so you fear it
There is wisdom so astonishingly simple
That you can't conceive of it

And so you don't understand me

Purity

Follow your heart they say
But do you know
The contents of your own heart?
How do you know the heart is free?
A heart that says, follow me
I will protect you
I will make you safe
You will be loved
You will be admired

This heart is muddled in fear
And slave to ego
Follow it nowhere

A heart that says to you
Follow me if you choose
I will show you wonder
To open you to all of creation
I will show you beauty
And joy and laughter

I will bring you peace within the storm
I will show you the perfection in chaos
I will teach you how to honor yourself
And how to honor your other selves

I will bring you hope
From the core of your being
So that you may learn to love
I will bring you freedom
That you may choose to love

I will bring you all these things
And set them before you
And I will tell you that you must choose them
Every moment of every day
For the rest of your life

If your heart says these things to you
Follow it to the ends of the earth
Follow it beyond the stars
Follow it into the mind and heart of God
For that is where it will lead

Just for a Moment

Leave the smallness behind
Smallness is an open grave
That begs you, 'come hither'
Smallness is a prison cell
Where meals
Are delivered on time

The Earth rolls out a carpet
Of green before you
And the stars a crown
And you think
you know what you are
And you seek in vain
For freedom from your own
Delusion of smallness
It can never be

For just a moment
Let yourself fall
Into the heart of the world
Let it embrace you
And nourish you
As your essence
Not the desolate creature
You pretend to be

Life can feed you
Or life can bleed you dry
How shall it be?

You are the starlight
And yet you stub your toe
And curse the darkness
You are the awesome dread
Of an approaching storm
And yet a crack of thunder
Makes you catch your breath

The wonder is not
That you are so wondrous
But that you can think
You are so small
And believe in reflections
In mirrors

While your mind
Is wrapped in pettiness
Your heart
Is soaring with the wind

It has always been so
And you do not know this
Because you cannot know
You can only sense it's endlessness
It's openness and boundlessness
It's vulnerable tender freedom
Hopelessly unconstrained
And undirected
And this frightens you

It frightens me too
But just a moment
Is enough
There are journeys
From which one never truly returns
Quite the same

I wish you bon voyage

Lovolution

With fiery passion and purpose
The glory of conquest
Love is a lusty bed

With dignity and honor
And mutual fulfillment
Love is a contract

With gentle heart
And adoring eyes
Mirror images to be cherished
Love is a reflection

When all the petals have fallen
And the dagger's dread divides
And dreams have turned to dust
And the wrenching crack
Of thunder
Splits the heart asunder

When one finally knows
What love is not
Then does love awaken
Within the shattered heart of self

Always has one sought
The face of love
Through the eyes of passion
Grasped with needy fingers
Embraced in illusion
How could it not
But slip away?

Love cannot be sought
For one has become the beloved
And needs it not

Oh, but heaven is not done
For that which is love
Draws to it love
In splendorous reflection
It has always been so
Don't you see?

How does love
Find remorse in being?
Why would love
Seek it from other?
There can be no sorrow
Where there is nothing but
Love....being

Soul Shadows

What is freedom
But wholeness?
What is soul
But wholeness divided
Split from Singularity
The birth of multiplicity
Seeking Unity
Within the hopeless tangle
Of it's own
Broken heart?

Illusions don't surrender
At death's door
For death is but a stone
To mark the passage
Of time
And time but the movement
Of shadows
And shadows but the blocking
Of the sun
And the sun but a child
Of the Light

As long as the Light shines
Upon a single soul
A shadow is cast
And in this shadow
Universes are born.....
And even in stillness
Longing seeks Wholeness

All shadows are illusions
Even soul shadows

You ARE

In the beginning
There was nothing
And it's still there!
Pure Awareness
Timeless spaceless
Infinite potential

What becomes of infinite
Potential
Outside the constraints of time?
Everything of course!

In the silence of nothingness
In the aloneness of Singularity
A single thought
In the mind of God
Who AM I?.......

This wondrous thought
Exploded Singularity
Into infinite multiplicity
And rang out to infinity
Creating universes in it's wake
In an instant of timeless
Perfection

Consciousness was born
And with it a dream
And through the dream
The eyes of God
Turn upon itself
And know it's own wonder

The dreamer
Must become the dream
Or it cannot be so

Don't you know?
You placed the stars
In the heavens
That you could stand in awe
At your own reflection

You set the sun ablaze
To delight in dappled shadows
You set the moon aglow
To dream of your tomorrows
The thunderous ocean waves
Speak to you
Of your own secret power

The empty place in your heart
Has a purpose as well
It tells a tale of home
Look very deeply
Into that nothingness
And stay very still
And you just might
Catch a glimpse
Of the face of God

Ignorance Rides

Ignorance blunders, plunders, stumbles
And rights itself again, head high
Pretending it was a gesture done for emphasis
But he is loved in his ignorance
Because it is all a part of awakening
From the dream

Ignorance babbles rabbles scrabbles
Pounces pronounces denounces
Weighs sautés delays
And still he is loved
Because a mirror must reflect
Or how would one ever notice oneself?

Ignorance crucifies, justifies, demonize
In your eyes in your face in your space
Demanding, commanding, branding
And still he is loved
For he is no other
Than my own sacred Self

Ignorance rides a white horse
And brandishes a sword of Truth
And all must bow
To the fool with the sword

And still he is loved
And Soul is honored
And a candle is lit
To the heart of God
That beats in the chest
Of an ignorant fool

Breath of Love

All such things
As love will bring
In the journey of the soul
In the hour of remembrance
As a breath
As a summer breeze
A divine exhale
Then drawing inward
That which escapes
Our failing sight
Into the cauldron of self
To be distilled, Purified
And breathed into the world
Once more

Such is love
Bridging chasms
Breaching barriers
Lighting up the dark spaces
Between thyself and thou
Love seeking love
Where love seems not to be

Love's passion
Makes it so
And so it shall be

A Glint of Steel

Truth and passion
Are as lovers
Each seeking
To embrace the other

The sword of truth
Is forged
In the fires of passion
And cuts clean
The ties that bind
The soul from flight

Loves feathery touch
Soothes the tortured soul
But the sword of Truth
Shall set it free

Yin and yang
Is the dance of love
Only wisdom knows
The choiceless choice
When to swing the blade
And when to keep it in it's sheath

Loves gentle touch
Should not tarry long
When the glint of steel
Slices through the air

Is this love?
Oh, yes, my gentle one
For Love and Truth
Are one and the same
Forever wedded
In the 'I' of God

Wordless Moments

The world is far more graceful and magical
Than we would have it in our more lucid moments
Do you know that a poem can occur in a single moment?
That moment is my poem
Wordless and magnificent
A moment we struggle in vain
To capture and tame
In symbols and lines
Such nonsense!

Never mind the words
They will never capture a moment
Just silently wait for the next

They're like droplets of dew
Falling from the trees
Catching glints of sun on the way down

They're careless and free
And so you too must be
Just let them be......Let them be

The Quickening

I can't tell you what it is
For I don't know myself
But it would have me tell you
There is no more time to waste

The moment is at hand
Your toes grip the ledge
The wind is stiff
The sun beckons
Your wings are strong
The Earth reaches for your ankle

Take the time to look back
Over your shoulder
And you will turn to stone
There is no more time
Now....What will you do?

I think you know

Always have you been seen
I think you know
From the first glance
That told a tale
Beyond words and thought

There is a gathering of man
I think you know
Threaded by a silver chord
We meet in our dreams
And conspire with God
To bring light to darkness

Some are warriors
I think you know
Some inspire love
With words of wonder
Some go where angels
Fear to tread

Every now and then
I think you know
The chord draws us near

This is for you
See you in your dreams
Namaste my friend

Just a Dream

Life's greatest mystery
Is that there is no mystery
God plays a joke on us
And many lifetimes later
.....We laugh

Mountains are climbed
To summits bare
Rivers crossed
And crossed again
And finally we come to rest
In that chamber in the heart

We take the summits
And rivers with us
And peace prevails

How could we know
It was too simple
For the mind to grasp?
How could we know
That freedom rises
From the ashes of self?

When the doing is done
And the thoughts wear thin
And the dark night is over
And there's nothing left to lose
The moment is ripe
To awaken from the dream
.......That never was

Requiem for a Lover

When your heart cannot be broken anymore
And God has brought you to your knees
And ripped your heart from your chest
And your life drained from your wound
Did you think that you would die?
What was the experience like?

Did your heart burst with a love
Unmeasured and ungrasped
Terrifying in it's power
As though more than a glimpse
Would snuff your miserable existence
In it's own name?
And how could it matter?

Was there a gentle presence?
Something that has always loved you
Always been present
Unchanging and unchanged
And you simply never noticed?
Did God give you your life back?

It was by your request
What if you had not insisted?
What was the experience like?
What if you had surrendered everything to love
In that sacred moment?
Would the experiencer have died
As you were so sure you would?

Or would love have given birth to Self
.....as love?

Full Circle

Wind whistling through the trees
Rose Quartz
Endless starry skies
The smell of a summer night
Wafting through my bedroom window

Oh to have the simple wonder
The unchained thoughts
The unfettered heart
Of a foolish child
In a world still too big
To fit in a shoe box

Just once more God
I promise I won't be careless with it
This time

Deception

Opinions are disavowed
When riddled with such obscurity
And interrogative delicacy
As to escape the tender embrace
Of the author
Of such burnt offerings

Language obtains
Such subtlety of purpose
So it seems
When words are victimized
Ripped from the throat
Made meaningless
By the very act
Of speaking them aloud

And yet they remain
As is plainly seen
Battered and broken
Struggling to form
A consonant chord
In the vacuum
Meant to suck angels
Through the tiny opening
That remains at our core

But all it does
Is empty the soul
Of all that it loves
And keeps it buried to the neck
In the very ground we've grown to detest

Such emptiness there is here
As to rob the songbird
Of it's song

Longing

The mind stands alone
In the barren wasteland
Starving, hungry for new thoughts
Thirsty for new knowledge
That will finally release it
From it's dreary endless search

It wants to know why
Yet all it can say is how
It wants to be free
Yet all it knows to do
Is build prisons

It searches, endlessly searches
But finds nothing to eat
Nothing to drink
Nothing to breathe but stale air

Then one day in despair
The mind asks a question
What is this longing
That is not of the mind?
Where does it come from
And why is it not mine to answer?

And then comes the silence
A silence filled with nothing
But longing
The walls so carefully built
Begin to crumble and fall
And beyond those walls
Is a deep ocean of possibility
And the heart turns it's gaze
On that deep ocean
And takes it's first breath
From the deep ocean of life
Nourishes itself
On the deep ocean of wonder
Quenches it's thirst on
The deep ocean of love

Suddenly, the spell is broken
And the mind admits defeat
And the heart speaks at once
To both the mind
And the deep ocean
From which they both sprang
The connecting link
Between mind and source of mind
Heart and source of heart
Love and source of love

The tide begins to turn
Ah I see
The mind never knew the ocean
The heart never left the ocean
It always sat on the shore
And patiently waited for a voice
For a question
What is this longing
And why is it not mine to answer?

I AM

You are the expression of life
In all it's forms and complexity
You are the vastness itself
And the emptiness it contains
The nothingness
That makes the fullness possible
The here and now
That makes infinity and eternity possible

You are the thought
That forms time and space
And locks itself within

There is nothing to find
You are already IT
There is nowhere to go
Everywhere you go, there You are
You are always
The still, silent center
Of your own creation

Submerging yourself in the here and now
Must awaken you from your dream
This is the axis on which you spin
The webs of self deception
You are the freedom you seek
And so you see
There is no-one to set free

Meditating on Duality

Hard as rose quartz
Soft as eider down
Thick as molasses
Thinner than a breath
Bright as the noonday sun
Black as a starless sky
Gut wrenching love lost
New love beckoning

And then the silence............
And none of it ever mattered

Good Grief!

Grief is a sham
A trickster
Demand to have a look
Up the sleeves
And behind the back

A thought in the mind
A whisper on the wind
Retention on the retina
An echo from the hillside

Can the absence of something
Bring sadness?
Well.....yes.
The heart clings to loss
As the morning dew
Clings to a blade of grass
Until the sun shines
And it fades into mist

Relish your grief
Wallow in it
For as long as you choose
It is only the dark side......
Of joy

Wild Stallion

Hooves pounding
Ground shaking
Strength flashing
Chest heaving
Eyes glistening
Mane waving
Beauty stalking
Sinews stretching
Pride knowing
Honor demanding
Elegance seething
Freedom laughing

Peace

Blue skies happen now
Cloud shrouded mountain peaks
Mist rising from a placid pond
Where ducks paddle and dip
And ghosts of frogs plop
Making concentric circles
That play with the morning light

Where was peace yesterday?
Squalls raging
All about me
Seeking to invade me

Ha! 'Twas just a dream
Of something that needed to be done
That's all it ever was......
I'll be damned!

Saving Worlds

And there it is
The wide eyed struggle
Self righteous insistence
That God is a fool

A mistake has been made
And we must rescue
The hapless creator
From his carelessness

Nothing has gone wrong
Fear is but the search for love
Struggle seeks surrender
Indifference seeks compassion
Arrogance seeks humility
Sadness seeks joy
Violence seeks peace
Separation seeks unity
Aloneness seeks oneness

In your deepest heart
You know this to be so
Or you would not be here

Freedom is borne of misery
And is birthed from within
And tempered by
The fires of hell
I beg of you
To let it be

Mirrorred Facets

There is but One jewel
In all it's wondrous aspects
A world of reflections
Sacred pools of light
In which is cast forth
The heart of hearts
That beats deep in thy chest

As that heart stands before you now
Naked and brilliant
Bold as Truth
It has always been so
Peer deeply into those eyes
Tell me if it be friend or foe

Come closer still
And see thine own reflection

Star Quest

When mind releases it's boundaries
It becomes egotistical and vain
But when heart lets go it's bounds
..It becomes boundless

It takes within itself
All that was once outside
And breathes passion from the air
It lets itself be carried by the wind
To plummet with the rain
To dance among the stars
And count them among it's confidants

It leaves smallness behind
For minds to dissect
And make smaller still
Minds that can't breathe
In their hollow spheres

Do you want your heart
To race with the wind
And chase the clouds
And watch the Earth
Spin silently in space?

Then loosen it's shackles
Unlock it's cage
And set it free!

Let it peer through the eyes of God
And cast it's shadow across the sky
In all it's arrogant plunder
And bring you the gold
From it's star quest!

Ghost Ship

Mind floats in a vibrant peace
In a vacant sea of nothingness
It fills the sea with churning water
And terrified that it may drown
It builds a vessel to float upon the sea
And fearing that it may be lost at sea
It builds a sail and fills it with wind
And fearing the wind it builds a galley
And cowers below deck......
Trembling.....
Imprisoned by it's own creations

Born Free

The lion seeks nothing
But to be the heart and soul
Of a lion
And in this he is blessed
With the courage of a warrior
The stature of a king
The grace of a ballerina

It is from that sacred place
By being that which it is
In it's heart of hearts
That freedom reigns

Gratitude

Tears of gratefulness
Are the river of life
That joins a mountain stream
To it's home in the ocean

It's the silver thread
That binds one to other
In a sacred dance
A secret longing
To dissolve the boundaries
Between thyself and thou

Wipe away the bitter tears
If you must
But bring on the river of life
And watch your heart dance
The sunlit rippled waters
To your home in the sea

Ungodly Fantasies

Mind is the maker of illusions
God is not an illusion
The riddle will never be solved
God will not be captured and tamed
By logic and reason
Or kept within the straight jacket
Of ideas and words

God is not free
Not loving, joyful, peaceful
You have been lied to
Santa Clause and the tooth fairy never existed
And all children come to know this
When the time is right

God is the essence of freedom itself
But without that from which freedom is sought
God is joy itself
Having forgotten what joy is not
God is peace itself
Long since deaf to the sounds of clashing swords
God is love itself
Infinitely more than mind can conceive
More than the human heart can ever hold
More than a universe of creation
Could ever express

Truth by Dawn

Mind would have it that life
Is but a problem to be solved
Mind is the maker of monsters
Out of moonlit shadows
Dancing on the walls

The soothing hoot of the night owl
Becomes the mournful dirge
Of the walking dead
As the gentle wind
That brushes the lilac against the eaves
Becomes a dreadful intruder

In the revealing light of the rising sun
All such beast that prowl and prey
Return to the pit of evil
To await the twilight's gloom

Or is it the light of truth
Set alight on the wings of the morning dove
That brought freedom to the heart
And stilled the mind of it's foolishness?

Truth

Truth is that which makes you angry.....
Just before it sets you free
Truth is that which shatters your dreams
And fills you with wonders
That you could never have dreamed

Truth is that which calls you a liar to your face
Robs you of everything you think you know
And replaces it with knowing

Truth is that which brings you to your knees
And rips the darkness from your heart

Truth is that which empties you completely
To make room for the smallest portion of Grace

Truth is an open plain
With no boundaries in sight
The salty scent of the ocean
Carried on the wind
That tells you your getting close

The scent of roses
That reminds you of your first love
Truth is the touch of a lover
That brings you to tears

Truth is always bigger than you are
Always wider and deeper
But oh so silent and peaceful

Fall in love with Truth
And let it break your heart

Positively Insane

Positive thinking is the absurdity
Of mind choosing to think
Something other than
What it chooses to think
As if there are two choosers

It's the layering of more resistance
To hide the resistance that's already there
Like covering the warning light
On your dashboard with electrical tape

It's ultimately the pretense of choice that says
'I am the controller of my life
And I'm going to prove it even if it kills me!'
Which of course..... it will

God Advises the Poet

Feel free to pack your bags
And schedule your connections
You're not going where you think you are
You're going where the words take you
And thank God for that

You're not leading your muse
You're following it
Don't grab it by the wings
And drag it into your tiny world
Let go of your own

The poem is always found in the same place
And it's never where you are
If it were it would keep you there
And then it would have failed

It's always found beyond the boundaries
Of your own ignorance
It's there to teach you
That such boundaries are only in your mind

Be grateful for the beauty that surrounds you
And notice that a thought cannot contain it
Be grateful for the longing
That has you sniffing the air
For a fresh scent of freedom
Be grateful for the village idiot
Because you still have a mind
That needs to be reminded
That you need not be one

Freedom

Everything in God's universe is free
It's the needing of it
That makes it seem not so
The mere thought
That something is missing
Is all that prevents wholeness
From completing our lives
At once the freedom of man
And man's greatest curse

Between the curse and the freedom
We are being lived

Who Are You?

There is a moment
In an endless chain of moments
When a spark of light
Can understand that question

At that very moment
The answer is out of reach
And the journey home has begun

The child who asks itself that question
Never ceased to be a spark of light
And yet images appear
And thoughts arise
And hands grasp
And it all seems.....quite reasonable

That which grasps cannot be the grasping
The eye that sees cannot be the eye that's seen
The thought that arises cannot be the thinker
For how could anything see itself
Without standing outside itself?
And if it is outside
How can it be inside?
And so you see
All that you see
Tells you only
What you could never be

You reside so deeply behind the eyes
That you are invisible
So deeply within the myriad thoughts
That you are unthinkable

You are the seeing itself not the seer
You are the thought itself not the thinker
You are the awareness that makes it possible
To be aware of such marvelous insanity

Now don't you feel foolish
For taking it all so seriously?

Bewilderment

Once the path was clear
There was a time I knew
What needed to be done
What had always been done
What my father did
And his father before him

Though I struggled with it
As all free spirits must
Somehow I always knew
Once the path was clear
Even when it was not easy
And the rains came
And the nights grew long
And foreboding

I learned to lean on solid things
And to bend without breaking
I learned to tune my strings
To the melody that I heard
Through my window
From the streets

I found my notes
The ones I could play well
And the ones best left unstruck
Still I always knew
What needed to be done

Once the path was clear
But now the forest sings a Different
Melody
And the sky speaks to me
From behind the clouds
Now the path has trailed off
And spreads wide to open fields

And empties into wide rivers
That flow into endless oceans
Reflecting an infinite sky
And my God where am I?

My mind wanders from port to
Valley to mountain top
Through the stars to nothingness
And back again to the sea
Looking for a reason to be

While my heart melts
Into the beauty
Of the simplest
Thoughtless moment
Where nothing is clear
Nothing is known
And nothing needs to be done

Grace

Grace is the blossoming of beauty
In most unexpected ways
A flower in the desert
The sunlit glint of the dewdrop
The liquid peace
Of the crashing ocean waves

Grace is the touch of the beloved
That melts the heart
The touch of God
That frees the soul at last
From it's long dark night

Grace is the perfection
That levels the oceans
And builds the mountains
And spins the wistful arms of galaxies
In perfect harmony
To stretch our wonder
And open our hearts
To unthinkable possibilities
That can only be felt

Grace is a name we give
To that which pulls us forward
Patiently waiting
For the sweet surrender
Just beyond our reach
Yet closer than our breath

Integrity

How can all things not
Be speaking to You?

To live with integrity
Is to walk in one direction
At a time Instead of two

To stride boldly
To where you are
Clearly going anyway
How could it be simpler?

To look with integrity
Is to seek
The hidden secrets within
And notice the shimmering
Reflection of self
In the eyes
Of each beloved stranger
In the wonder of a starry night
In the peace of dappled
Shadows

To listen with integrity
Is to hear the voice of God
From behind the veils of mind
And to seek that source
In the song bird
And rustling leaves

To be integrity
Is to be exactly what you are in
This moment
Having forgotten
That there must be a better way

It is to heal the rift of mind
That reaches out
For God with one hand
And pushes away with the other

To heal the rift of heart
That hides from it's own darkness
And pretends it's not afraid
Of the dark
The crack of thunder and the
Howling wind
The things that go 'bump'
In the Night

To walk with integrity
Is to honor that which you value
By living it in your bones
By letting it live you
And knowing deeply
There is no other way to live
And embrace what You ARE

Integrity is far too simple
For the mind to grasp
End the need to be
What you are not

Is that too high a price to pay
To ransom yourself
From your own prison?

The Secret

Miserable mankind
Endlessly struggles
For moments of joy
While the rose happily grows
Where it is planted

Miserable mankind
Works tirelessly for peace
While the stream flows
Gracefully to the sea

Miserable mankind
Is rarely inspired
To greatness and beauty
While nature
Knows no other way to be

Nature knows a secret
Which miserable mankind has forgotten
Life is a gift received with open arms
Rather than a closed fist

Life is a singular harmonious jewel
Reflecting it's own endless beauty
In every individual facet
Rather than the harsh glint
Of the shattered pieces
Of a broken vase

Nature rejoices in it's joy
Is at peace with it's own harmony
Is inspired by it's own beauty
Nature is in love with the simplicity
Of being

Yin and Yang

How would you have it be
Knowing the fickle nature
Of your own mind and heart?
Restless movement from light to shadow
The need to be wherever you are not
And return again

Can you imagine perpetual spring
With never a first snow
The crispness of the cold air
Ice crystals and frozen ponds

How long would it take
For the blossoming spring
To meet the dullness
Of your careless mind
And lose it's miracle?

You have a mind that forever walks the line
That divides the world in two
And creates a perpetual movement
From one to the other and back

It's your mind that brings
The soft twilight stillness
To the hard shadows of day

It's you who becomes drowsy
From an old summer
And brings on winter's slumber

It is you who contemplates your walls and fences
Then casts your boundaries
To the infinite starry starry night

It's all exactly
As you have created it to be
And it's all happening inside of You

Knowing this
Is the birth of peace

Saving The World

The world spins on it's own axis
The moon and stars slip silently
Across an unmarked sky
Galaxies forming the very space
Which they inhabit

Clouds cry
And rivers run to the sea
And the Lilly awakens from it's slumber
In answer to some unseen alarm clock

And man can stand amidst this wonder
And not be overcome in awe
Of it's self perpetuating perfection
And not be humbled by it's secret knowingness

His arrogance revealed
In harmony that he can only mimic
Beauty that he can only surrender to
Wisdom that he can only dream of

The world does not need saving
This is what the owl has been preaching
This is why the Earth shakes
The smug smiles from our faces
Why the ocean swallows our homes
And stakes it's own claim

A thousand miracles a second
Are happening inside your body
And you have nothing at all to do with it
Let it be
For God's sake let it be

Both Sides Now

What once was a battle of honor
Fought with courage for country and King
Is now a battle for justice and freedom
From the tyranny of that same King
And the line that once divided
Oppressed and oppressor
So clear upon the battle field
Has faded in the heart
And the warrior has lost
His taste for blood

Pride

Pride is a gift of honor to other
That is never released from one's grip
Pride is not acceptance
Any more than moonlight on the water
Is the moon itself

Pride is the snowflake
And guilt the bitter wind
That forms it's crystalline beauty
The darkness cannot be ripped from the night
As wetness is forever wed to water

How is one to lay claim to pride
For the perfection
Of God's graceful wonder
Without chaining oneself
To the anchor of guilt
For God's fallen angels?

The heart bursting with pride
Is likewise pierced
With a gleaming dagger of guilt
As the wind is mistaken
For one's own breath

Variations of Love?

Perhaps so
Once the mental combine
Has had it's way with it
Beheading waves of grain
Separating wheat from chaff
Valuing one, discarding the other

The miracle of this wondrous invention
Is it's relentless drive
To split one into two
Then to seek wholeness
Among the carnage

And another miracle
No less astounding
As Love's ineffable Singularity
Touches mind's duplicity
And Love is split asunder
Though Love be honored
Fear is given birth

To paint Love with the mind
Is an error borne of fear
For something is given life
To act as the canvas
On which it must be painted

Happiness

The welcome visitor
Bearing gifts of joy
Is equally your bitter enemy
As on a whim, he abruptly rises
Gathers his gifts and steals away
Like a thief in the night

Your robber was your own guest
And it's not the first time
Nor will it be the last
Until you finally see the love
Unrequited

The sleepless nights planning
The phone calls in the dark hours
A most delightful banquet laid
All to entice your guest to return
Knowing that he will rob you blind
Because it is his nature to return
To the emptiness from which he came

A fraud, a pretense
At best a compromise
A warm fire to stave the cold and dark

Bolt your doors and close the blinds
Refuse to play the game
And know that Love is a gift
That is given to oneself in the solitude
Born of sweet surrender
And forged in painful remembrance

Know that Peace is a gift
Arising within a gentle heart
That has lost it's way so many times
It's ready to call wherever it is, home

Know that Joy is a gift
That arrives at the door unbidden
Because it can no longer resist
The warmth and comfort
The loving peace
That simmers quietly and humbly
Within

Choosing

Choosing is the rustling of the leaves
Playing to a tune of an unseen wind
The painted smile
That hides the secrets
Of a tortured heart
The mirrored reflection of vanity
Mistaken for preeminence

Out of that which you have been
Arises what you are
And from such innocent being
Desire flows unbidden
To the surface of the pool of mind

If willingness should follow
In it's current
It is already done

Mind, feeling the change in the air
Fearing that it is not the source
Will call upon the wind
To bow to it's bidding
That it might declare itself
Prince of the sea once more

The sea knows of delusions
And suffers such fools gladly
All things are permitted
To arise and fall back
Into it's loving embrace

Mirrors

Reflections of Source
Reflect as source
The creatures of the forest
Untamed beauty and flowing grace
Play also the game of predator and prey
Much like the rapturous beloved
Who once broke your heart

The thorn in the rose
The enchanting darkness
The freedom of a wind struck sea
The glory of war
The comfort of fire
Bittersweet pain

A swiftly moving river resists nothing
And this is what makes it what it is
Stand against it, and you cannot but fall
That which resists nothing
Is unstoppable

The world is our mirror
Reflecting vanity
Answering the question
Who is the fairest one of all?
Did you think it was happening
Outside of you?

To My Love

Love paints it's own portrait
In the image of the beloved
Seen so clearly now
In the reflecting pool
In the deep regions of my own heart

On your lips I paint the perfect words
To bring courage to uncertainty
On your cheeks a childlike wonder
Innocent and fresh to awaken my own
And in your eyes I paint the deepest ocean
A portal straight to your own heart
Unfailing love

The stars are in their places
Because we are together
God has opened a door
Because we have knocked
The moon lights our way
Because we walk toward it
This is the power of love

I love you as gentle things must be loved
If they are to remain so
I love you as wild things are loved
Untamed and free
I love you as graceful things are loved
With an eye for beauty

If there is even a space between us
There is also a bridge that forms
How can I know anymore
Where your love ends
And mine begins?
You are my portrait
And I am yours
Thank you for that

Creation

A passing thought in the mind of God
And the flutter of angel wings
Ringing out through Nothingness
Like a pebble in a pond
Like waves of time
Crashing the shores of space
Leaving universes in it's wake

Deaf and mute a Singularity split
And lovers embrace
In the pale moonlight

A nod of the head and a wink of the 'I'
And a child is born
And suckled to the breast

As the wispy arms of galaxies spin
And the clock tics
And the sound of childish laughter
Rings out through the heavens
Like a pebble in a pond
Like waves of love
Crashing the shores of emptiness

Flowing

Can you see how it all flows for them
And how we can't seem to get it right?
How the aspen shakes off the wind
In a shimmering dance of surrender?
How the hawk faces up to it
Hovering in place for the sheer joy of flying?

Do you see how the vine climbs
Because it can and
Not because it has to?
How the flower follows the sun across the sky
Like an adoring lover?

Notice how the river plays with the rocks
And sings into crevices
And babbles about nothing at all
As it effortlessly flows wherever it's going

Ask the aspen if it has a grudge with the wind
Or the hawk if it thinks it's going somewhere
Ask the vine what it expects to find
When it reaches the top of the world
Warn the flower of it's co-dependent tendencies
Tell the river there is danger around the bend

That's our job, you know
To remind them of what could happen to them
If they ever stopped flowing

Soul to Soul

Just behind your eyes
There's someone I need to talk to
But you keep looking away
I listen for a familiar voice
But you keep screaming over it
And it's hard to hear

Your heart is my heart
But you keep the doors closed
And I can't breathe
Every time we get up to dance
You think you need to lead
And then you step on my feet

There is a visitor inside you
That I need to be with
You think I've come to see you
And so you slam the door in my face

I slam my door in return
So here we sit
Behind closed doors
Trying to understand
How we became two
....And what to do?

Undone

Spinning tales of wanderlust
Time weaving together thoughts
Filling everything with love and fear
Joy and sorrow
Any fabric will do

But of all the stories written
There is one that begins in desire
And ends in death
It breathes on it's own
And writes itself onto your tombstone
The story to end all stories

One day, the Earth will move
And won't let you stand
All so carefully woven, tears open
Leaving gaps in the perfect story
Of me

Run, avert your eyes, pull together the threads!
Pretend you are insane!
It's too late
You've seen what lies
Beneath the story of your life
The dark and empty vacuum
Of nothingness
No past or future
The foolish lies that life has told

It can't be undone.....ever
You have been undone

Sanctuary

The dreamer finds purpose in his nightmares
Or why would they be?
A chalice filled with bitterness
Is better than emptiness
And less in need of gratitude
Than sweetness

Sanctuaries are prisons
Darkened to the eyes of danger
Stale air still and suffocating
The candle flame dying

Tear down the curtains
Throw open the door
And let the beast devour you
Once the fresh air fills the lungs
And the eyes adjust to the light
And you have been consumed
You will know love has been stalking you

What else could it be?
Love knows nothing of sanctuary

Enough!

What is the sense in floating away on a funeral pyre
When where I am going is to my birthday celebration?
A pathway across the sky, deep into the darkness
And lit by the brightest star in the heavens

How can I mourn a single passing moment of timelessness?
How dare I turn a sullen face to God
As if I know something of life that I must show Him?
My only hope is in hopelessness?
This is a dirge and I'll not sing that song

The wind is whistling a tune as it rustles the leaves
The river is giggling at my foolishness
The ocean is roaring with laughter
The very idea that anything could ever be lost by gaining eternity

The terrain has become too much like desert for my tastes
And I don't want someone to find me here
Looking for something I brought with me
I'll be in the forest playing tag with the squirrels
Swimming in the rivers and watching the sun set through the ferns

If God wants me
He knows where to find me

Reflections

Does the hawk curse the air
Or the fish, water?
Did Van Gogh resent the canvas
Or Mozart the piano?
Has darkness armed itself
For battle with the light?

Or is it the cutting edge of mind
Dreaming a dream of otherness
And frightening itself
With it's own reflection?

Freedom

Freedom is wherever you are not
And if you are not
There is no need of freedom
Tis a rainbow that runs
Only as fast as you can chase it
And stays only as long as the rain

One is the Truth.
Love is the melody it sings to itself
That the dancers be entranced
And lose themselves in the dance

To stand in the shadow of your greatest fear
Is to know your own courage
Bold, red strokes of passion
Painted on a canvass of midnight black

How else would you have it?
How else could it be?

Vanishing

Starless night
Nothingness forever
Blinding me
Roaring waves
Deafening me
Sand beneath my feet
Slipping me out to sea
Rain pelting me
Melting me
Then a flash
Then a crack of thunder....

Why?

Isn't it you
Who plows your fields and sows your seeds
That you might know abundance?

Isn't it you
Who waits at dusk for a painted sky
That you might know beauty?

Isn't it you
Who seeks the beloved behind every pair of eyes
That you might know love?

Why?
Why do you move at all?
What is the source of hope
And your longing to be free
And to paint the bold strokes of courage
Upon your own canvass?

Now you know
Why you must cry

Trying to Hold the Ocean

How many moons has Jupiter?
How far is Sirius anyway?
How many miles in a light year?

To even ask
Is to squeeze the infinity
Of an endless starry, starry night
Into the palm of your hand
And erase the wonder from your heart

How tall is that mountain?
What is that rose called?
Is it time for the swallows
To return to Capistrano?

Do you see how if the wood cutter has his way
Everything will become small enough
To be consumed in the stove
Or at least stacked neatly in the shed
For a cold day that may never come?

Don't let the bright crimson of the setting sun
Keep you from noticing
A beauty that you can never own
A wonder that you can never understand
A power that you can never wield

Never be the dancer
Always the dance
Never the listener
Always the music

You would not treasure
The broken shards of a shattered vase
You cannot keep the moonlight
In your pocket
Or the ocean
In the palm of your hand

Thought cages
(In response to 'Why the caged bird sings' by Maya Angelou)

The freedom of flight, grace and glory, yes
The song of joy, yes
All duly noted, appreciated and honored,
But all witnessed through eyes covered over
By a smear of indignation
Eyes read by a mind thinking far too much
Of it's own fate

What is not seen is the simplicity
Of the caged bird's willingness to be present
For it's incarceration
In the moment there is no suffering
Suffering is always waiting down river, around the bend
It is never where you are
It is not in the cage with the bird

Why would a caged bird sing?
Because it's not smart enough to know
That it is supposed to be suffering
From the weight of it's own thoughts
Cast into an imaginary future

The bird sings in desperation?
It has no desperation and so you lend it your own
It is you own wings that rise to meet the sky
It is your own desperate song that rises from your throat
The humble bird knows nothing of your struggle
It sings it's joyful song from behind the bars
Uncertain whether it is she who is caged
Or if perhaps it is you

If you listen closely enough to her song
You too may rise

No Pity for the Dreamers

A bird in flight on a windy night
Gives pause to all that matters

To all who brave the wrath of God
And dance while moonlight shatters
And falls like daggers come the dawns
That splinter when they break
To cast a spell....but tend to dwell
A moment in it's wake

Crystal sounds of winter nights
A petal in the snow
Lost in dreams of summers bright
And basking in the glow

To solitude that lets us dream
To hope that sets us free
To the lion in the city
And the prisoner on the open sea

You're everything that matters
You're all that matters to me

Somebody

Is it so bad to be a melody
Reverberating in the ears of the Beloved?
Is it so bad to be a whisper
Of wind through the trees?
Can you laugh and giggle
Burble and gurgle
As you flow around the rocks
And kiss the banks
Wind and wend you way
To the ocean's gaping mouth?

Can you be the elegance in the movement
The symmetry of expanding ripples
The 'plop!' of the frog
The scent of jasmine
A painted sky
A moonlit night
The space between the lips
Of a kiss

Is that enough for you?
Or do you need to be 'somebody'?

No Beginnings

In our hunger to know
We sift the shards
Of a silent past
And comb the wreckage
Of ancient dreams
Arranging what never was
On an impressive timeline
Leading to what always was
This precious moment
Not belabored
By great grandfathers
Nor dependent upon
The playful pranks
Of great grand children

In our desperation
We scan the skies for the One
Who surely must have set the
Wheel spinning
Cast a flame of mysterious
Properties
Onto a barren earth
And kissed a mighty kiss
That breathed life
Into our fiery skin

But I have seen
The sorcerer's magic
And it is not in the rubble of
Broken promises
Nor in the embrace of heaven

It is here
Closer than your own breath
It is now
In the magnificence
Of your own fertile mind
Peering through your telescope
As you spin
The wispy arms of galaxies

Digging the tar pits of imagination
As you unearth the bones
Of creatures that never were
Until you imagined them
Into existence

It is in your own precious heart
As you give birth to your own love
And nurture its wonder
And wonder in its innocence

You build the walls
That you may know
The end of separation
You set tyranny in motion
That you may know freedom
You conjure up broken hearts
That you may know
Your own compassion

The skies are full of stars
Because they delight you
The ground is full of memories
Because they comfort you
The mystery remains
Because you love mysteries

The 'Thing' Lives!

The stars will all burn out
The ocean will tire
Of crashing to the shore
The Earth's spin will turn
To a lazy wobble
And the wind will fall to the ground
And sleep
Before a thinker will surrender
His God given right
To be a thought

Yes!

God doesn't understand no
Why should the galaxies not spin
Or the stars number short of infinity?
A sun in supernova? Yes!
A black hole to suck the universe in
A piece at a time? Yes!
What wonder!
What a delight!

God will never tell you no
Dear God I am hungry and cold
Yes! You are!
Dear God my heart is breaking
Yes! It is!
Dear God I have the courage of a lion
The strength of a mountain
The passion of Sirius
And the heart of an angel
Yes!......You do!

It's the questions that matter
The answer is always the same
Yes!

Formless Form

There is no person
Who puts the thoughts in your head
Or sets your heart on fire
Who dreams the dream of you

You are the maker of worlds
The painter of the pictures
And this is your art
Your infinity dancing
Upon the head of a pin

It is more than enough
It is love that has pulled open
The shades of fear
Joy that has forgotten
The meaning of sorrow
Peace that is the axis around which
The violence of creation spins

You hold yourself
In the cradle of your hand
And wonder at your trembling
You set eternity upon a stage
And wonder at your mortality
You cast a shadow upon your pure joy
And wonder at your sorrow

But never was there a person
Just the reverberating echo
Of your own wonder

Bewildered and Free

In certainty lies delusion
And in delusion
Suffering humanity

Trade your certainty for bewilderment
Your ponderous knowledge
For wide eyed wonder
And your suffering
For liberation

You must die before you die

In the Beginning

You are the word
That spins the arms of galaxies
And set the sun ablaze
And teased the shadows
Out of murky ponds
And cast the seeds of eternity
Into the wind of infinity
And gave birth to mortality

You are the sound
That shakes the planet
And gives the stars their shimmer
The sound that opens hearts
That breaks and heals them

You are the word and the sound
But you are not that which has spoken
Only the echo
Slowly dying
As echoes do

Spinning

Moon waxes and wanes
Night turns to day
Summer to winter
Spiral arms of galaxies spinning
That mark time in aeons

Have you noticed
You're caught on the arms
Of some huge clock?

Yes I know
Sorrow is just the other side of joy
But have you wondered
Why it must be so?

Mind and Heart

Mind without heart is sterile
Heart without mind is sentimental

The pearl diver takes all to the depths
His courage and his wits
His wonder and his wisdom

One eye for beauty
And the other for clarity

Otherness

Only I... and here... and now
And a longing to fill the empty space
Between thyself and thou

A trick of light perhaps?
Half your face cast in shadow
That I cannot know and yet I must

A distorted reflection
As sunlit ripples on the pond
That I cannot see my features
And yet I must see

And so the movement begins
A dance with the wind upon the water
With the dappled shadows
With my own breaking heart

The Other Side of Something

You are still here to glimpse
This you know
And it is that knowing that you see
When you rub the sleep from your eyes

Not only can you not die
If you do not you cannot live
How delicious is that?

Deep sleep is the non-existence
From which you know existence
The nothingness from which you view thingness
The formlessness that gives form
The timelessness that tics the clock

You know nothing
But from your place of ignorance
You see nothing
But from blindness
Light arising from deepest darkness

How do you know that you know?
What is it that knows?
If it is you
Then it is you who must turn the coin
Then it is you who must pluck your eyes out
It is you who must die with the moonrise
That you may know the sunrise
There is no one to do this for you

All of it must happen before YOUR eyes
Or it does not happen at all
Do you see?

Phil Beaumont has a website where he explores happiness, inner peace and Truth in a secular, realistic, practical way with all who share the love of Truth.

www.RealizingHappiness.com

Made in the USA
Middletown, DE
10 April 2017